EMMANUEL JOSEPH

Digital Soulcraft: Blending Mental Wellness, Creativity, and Authentic Connection

First edition

This book was professionally typeset on Reedsy.
Find out more at reedsy.com

Contents

Contents

1

Chapter 1: The Dawn of Digital Soulcraft

The digital age has reshaped the way we live, but beneath the surface of screens and algorithms lies a deeper question: how do we preserve the soul in a world of constant connectivity? The dawn of digital soulcraft is not about rejecting technology but about reclaiming our humanity within it. It is about recognizing that our devices are not neutral tools; they shape our thoughts, emotions, and relationships. To craft a digital soul is to weave intention into the way we engage with the virtual world, ensuring that our inner lives remain rich and authentic.

At its core, digital soulcraft begins with awareness. We must notice the subtle ways technology influences our moods, our sense of time, and even our self-worth. The endless scroll of social media can erode attention, while the dopamine rush of notifications can tether us to shallow interactions. Yet, awareness transforms these forces into opportunities. By observing our digital habits, we can begin to design them with care, choosing practices that nurture rather than drain us.

This dawn is also a call to creativity. The digital realm offers unprecedented tools for expression, from writing platforms to visual art apps, but creativity requires more than access. It demands courage to share authentically, to resist the polished perfection that dominates online spaces. Digital soulcraft invites us to create not for applause but for connection, for the joy of shaping something that reflects our inner truth.

Finally, the dawn of digital soulcraft is communal. It is not a solitary pursuit but a collective awakening. As individuals learn to blend wellness, creativity, and connection, they ripple outward, inspiring others to do the same. The digital age, then, becomes not a threat to the soul but a canvas upon which we can paint new forms of human flourishing.

2

Chapter 2: The Weight of Constant Connectivity

The modern individual carries an invisible weight: the pressure of being constantly reachable. Emails, messages, and alerts blur the boundaries between work and rest, leaving little room for silence. This weight is not merely logistical; it is psychological. It fosters anxiety, a sense of never being enough, and a fear of missing out. Digital soulcraft begins by acknowledging this burden and daring to lighten it.

To lighten the weight, we must rediscover the value of disconnection. Silence is not absence but presence — the presence of our own thoughts, our own rhythms. When we step away from the constant buzz, we reclaim the ability to listen inwardly. This is not easy in a culture that equates busyness with worth, but it is essential for mental wellness. The soul needs pauses, just as music needs rests between notes.

Creativity thrives in these pauses. The mind, freed from the tyranny of notifications, begins to wander, to imagine, to connect disparate ideas. Many of history's great insights emerged not in moments of frantic activity but in quiet reflection. Digital soulcraft teaches us that creativity is not a luxury but a necessity, a way of processing the world and finding meaning within it.

Authentic connection also requires boundaries. When we are perpetually distracted, our relationships suffer. To be present with another person —

truly present — demands that we set aside the digital noise. In doing so, we affirm their value and our own. The weight of constant connectivity can be lifted, but only if we choose to carry less.

3

Chapter 3: The Inner Landscape of Screens

Screens are mirrors, reflecting not only information but also aspects of ourselves. They reveal our desires, our fears, and our longing for recognition. Yet, they can also distort, magnifying insecurities and reducing identity to curated fragments. The inner landscape of screens is complex, and navigating it requires honesty.

Honesty begins with admitting how screens affect us emotionally. The curated perfection of others' lives can spark envy, while the anonymity of online spaces can embolden cruelty. These reactions are not flaws but signals, pointing to deeper needs. Digital soulcraft asks us to listen to these signals, to understand what they reveal about our hunger for belonging, validation, or meaning.

Creativity offers a way to reclaim the screen as a canvas rather than a mirror. When we use digital tools to express rather than compare, we transform the landscape. A poem shared online, a sketch posted without fear of judgment, or a heartfelt message sent to a friend — these acts remind us that screens can carry authenticity as well as illusion.

Connection, too, is reshaped when we approach screens with intention. Instead of chasing likes or followers, we can seek genuine dialogue. A single conversation that touches the heart outweighs a hundred empty interactions.

The inner landscape of screens, then, is not fixed; it is crafted by the choices we make.

4

Chapter 4: Wellness in the Age of Algorithms

Algorithms promise efficiency, but they often trade our wellness for engagement. They feed us what keeps us scrolling, not what nourishes us. To practice digital soulcraft is to resist this manipulation, to reclaim agency over our attention.

Wellness begins with recognizing that our minds are not machines. They need rest, variety, and depth. Algorithms thrive on repetition, but the soul thrives on surprise. By curating our digital environments — choosing what we consume, limiting what drains us — we can align technology with our well-being.

Creativity becomes a form of resistance. When we create, we step outside the algorithm's predictions. We surprise ourselves and others, breaking the cycle of passive consumption. A digital painting, a journal entry, or a song recorded on a phone — these acts remind us that we are not merely data points but living beings with imagination.

Authentic connection also resists algorithmic reduction. Relationships cannot be quantified by metrics of engagement. They flourish in unpredictability, in the messy, unpolished moments that algorithms overlook. To craft a digital soul is to insist that wellness, creativity, and connection matter more than clicks.

5

Chapter 5: The Art of Digital Boundaries

Boundaries are not walls but invitations. They invite us to live with intention, to protect what matters most. In the digital age, boundaries are essential for wellness. Without them, we risk being consumed by the endless demands of connectivity.

Setting boundaries begins with clarity. We must ask ourselves: what do we value, and how do we want technology to serve those values? Boundaries might mean limiting screen time, turning off notifications, or designating tech-free spaces. These practices are not restrictions but freedoms, freeing us to live more fully.

Creativity flourishes within boundaries. Paradoxically, limits often spark innovation. When we step away from screens, we rediscover analog joys — sketching, writing by hand, walking in nature. These experiences feed our digital creativity, giving us fresh perspectives to bring back into the virtual realm.

Connection deepens when boundaries are respected. To give someone our undivided attention is a gift, and boundaries make that gift possible. Digital soulcraft teaches us that boundaries are not about exclusion but about presence, about choosing to be fully alive in each moment.

6

Chapter 6: The Rhythm of Attention

Attention is the currency of the digital age, and yet it is often spent carelessly. Notifications, headlines, and endless feeds fracture our focus into fragments, leaving us restless and unsatisfied. To practice digital soulcraft is to reclaim attention as a sacred resource, one that shapes the quality of our inner life.

Reclaiming attention begins with rhythm. Just as music requires tempo, our minds require patterns of focus and rest. By designing intentional rhythms — periods of deep work followed by genuine rest — we restore balance. This rhythm is not rigid but organic, attuned to the natural ebb and flow of energy throughout the day.

Creativity thrives when attention is rhythmic rather than scattered. A painter cannot complete a canvas in fragments of stolen seconds; they need immersion. Likewise, digital creativity requires spaces where attention is sustained. When we honor rhythm, we create conditions for ideas to bloom fully rather than wither prematurely.

Connection also deepens when attention is rhythmic. To give someone our full presence is to honor them, and this requires that we resist the pull of distraction. Digital soulcraft teaches us that attention is not merely personal but relational — the way we attend to others shapes the bonds we share.

7

Chapter 7: Silence as Sanctuary

In a world of constant noise, silence becomes a radical act. It is not emptiness but sanctuary, a space where the soul can breathe. Digital soulcraft insists that silence is not optional but essential, a practice that restores wellness and clarity.

Silence allows us to hear what is often drowned out: the subtle stirrings of intuition, the quiet voice of creativity, the unspoken needs of the heart. Without silence, we risk losing touch with ourselves, becoming echoes of the digital chorus rather than authors of our own lives.

Creativity blossoms in silence. The mind, freed from external chatter, begins to wander into uncharted territory. Ideas surface like fish in still water, shimmering with possibility. Silence is not passive; it is generative, a fertile ground for imagination.

Connection, paradoxically, is also strengthened by silence. To sit with another in quiet presence is a profound form of intimacy. In digital spaces, silence can mean resisting the urge to respond instantly, allowing depth to replace speed. Silence, then, is not withdrawal but communion.

8

Chapter 8: The Craft of Digital Storytelling

Stories are the threads that weave human experience, and in the digital age, storytelling has taken new forms. Blogs, podcasts, videos, and social media posts are all vessels for narrative. Yet, the craft of digital storytelling requires more than technology; it requires authenticity.

Authenticity begins with vulnerability. To tell a story that resonates, we must risk revealing ourselves. Digital platforms often reward polished façades, but true connection arises from honesty. A story of struggle, of imperfection, of growth — these are the narratives that touch hearts.

Creativity in storytelling is not about spectacle but about resonance. A simple anecdote, told with sincerity, can move more deeply than a grand production. Digital soulcraft invites us to craft stories that reflect our inner truth, stories that remind us and others of our shared humanity.

Connection is the ultimate purpose of storytelling. Stories bridge divides, allowing us to see ourselves in others. In digital spaces, storytelling becomes a way to counter isolation, to remind us that behind every screen is a soul longing to be understood.

9

Chapter 9: The Digital Commons

The internet is not merely a marketplace; it is a commons, a shared space where ideas, cultures, and communities converge. Yet, this commons is fragile, threatened by division, misinformation, and exploitation. Digital soulcraft calls us to steward the commons with care.

Stewardship begins with responsibility. Each post, each comment, each share contributes to the tone of the digital commons. When we choose kindness over cruelty, truth over distortion, we strengthen the fabric of this shared space. Responsibility is not abstract; it is enacted in daily choices.

Creativity enriches the commons. Art, music, writing, and dialogue shared online expand the collective imagination. The commons thrives when individuals contribute not only consumption but creation, offering gifts that inspire and uplift.

Connection is the lifeblood of the commons. It is not enough to coexist; we must engage. Dialogue, collaboration, and solidarity transform the digital commons from a marketplace of attention into a community of meaning. Digital soulcraft insists that the commons is ours to craft together.

10

Chapter 10: The Shadow Side of Digital Life

Every light casts a shadow, and the digital age is no exception. Alongside its gifts of connection and creativity lie dangers: addiction, isolation, and distortion. To practice digital soulcraft is to confront these shadows honestly, without denial or despair.

Addiction is one shadow. The design of digital platforms often exploits our psychology, hooking us into cycles of compulsive use. Recognizing this shadow is the first step toward reclaiming freedom. Awareness transforms addiction into an opportunity for intentionality.

Isolation is another shadow. Paradoxically, constant connectivity can leave us lonelier than ever, surrounded by interactions that lack depth. Digital soulcraft teaches us to seek quality over quantity, to prioritize relationships that nourish rather than drain.

Distortion is perhaps the most insidious shadow. The digital world can warp reality, spreading misinformation and magnifying extremes. Confronting this shadow requires discernment, the courage to question and the humility to learn. Shadows cannot be eliminated, but they can be integrated, becoming part of the craft of a digital soul.

11

Chapter 11: Creativity as Healing

Creativity is not merely an aesthetic pursuit; it is a form of healing. In the digital age, where stress and fragmentation often dominate, creativity becomes a balm for the soul. To craft something — a poem, a melody, a design — is to reclaim agency over chaos, to shape meaning from the raw material of experience.

Healing through creativity begins with permission. Too often, we silence ourselves with the belief that we are not "artists." Yet creativity is not about mastery but expression. A simple sketch, a journal entry, or a digital collage can carry profound therapeutic value. The act itself matters more than the outcome.

Digital tools expand the possibilities of healing creativity. Apps for music-making, platforms for sharing writing, and communities for visual art allow us to express ourselves in ways previously unimaginable. Yet the healing lies not in the technology but in the authenticity of the act. When we create honestly, we mend the fractures within.

Connection amplifies this healing. Sharing creative work, even imperfectly, invites others into our process. It reminds us that vulnerability is strength, that healing is communal. Digital soulcraft teaches us that creativity is not only personal medicine but also a gift to the collective.

12

Chapter 12: The Ethics of Digital Presence

Presence in the digital age carries ethical weight. Each post, each comment, each interaction shapes not only our own lives but the lives of others. Digital soulcraft insists that presence must be intentional, guided by values rather than impulse.

Ethical presence begins with honesty. Misrepresentation corrodes trust, while authenticity builds it. To be ethically present is to resist the temptation of curated perfection, to show up as we are. This honesty fosters wellness by aligning our digital selves with our inner truth.

Creativity also carries ethical responsibility. The stories we tell, the images we share, the art we produce — all ripple outward. Ethical creativity asks: does this uplift, does this harm, does this contribute to the commons? Digital soulcraft invites us to create with conscience, aware of the impact our work may have.

Connection is the heart of ethical presence. To engage respectfully, to listen as well as speak, to honor the dignity of others — these are ethical acts. In digital spaces, where anonymity can breed cruelty, choosing kindness becomes a radical form of soulcraft.

13

Chapter 13: Digital Rituals

Rituals anchor us, offering rhythm and meaning. In the digital age, rituals can transform our relationship with technology, turning it from distraction into devotion. Digital soulcraft invites us to craft rituals that nurture wellness, creativity, and connection.

Wellness rituals might include morning practices of mindful scrolling, evening digital fasts, or intentional pauses for reflection. These rituals remind us that technology is a servant, not a master. They restore balance, ensuring that our inner lives remain spacious.

Creativity rituals can be equally powerful. Setting aside time each day to write, sketch, or compose digitally creates a rhythm of expression. Rituals transform creativity from sporadic bursts into sustained practice, deepening our craft and enriching our souls.

Connection rituals strengthen relationships. Weekly video calls with loved ones, intentional messages of gratitude, or shared digital projects become sacred practices. Rituals remind us that connection is not accidental but cultivated, woven into the fabric of daily life.

14

Chapter 14: The Digital Body

Though technology often feels disembodied, our bodies remain central to digital life. Posture, eye strain, sleep disruption — these are physical consequences of digital engagement. Digital soulcraft insists that wellness must include care for the body.

Caring for the digital body begins with awareness. How do we sit, how long do we stare, how often do we rest? These questions matter. Wellness requires that we honor the body's needs, integrating movement, rest, and nourishment into our digital routines.

Creativity is embodied as well. The rhythm of typing, the gesture of drawing on a tablet, the cadence of speaking into a microphone — these are bodily acts. Recognizing the body's role in creativity deepens our appreciation of the craft.

Connection, too, is embodied. A smile on a video call, a tone of voice in a message, a pause before responding — these subtle bodily cues shape relationships. Digital soulcraft reminds us that even in virtual spaces, the body speaks.

15

Chapter 15: The Future of Digital Soulcraft

The future of digital soulcraft is not predetermined; it is crafted by our choices. As technology evolves, so too must our practices of wellness, creativity, and connection. The question is not whether technology will change but whether we will shape it with soul.

Wellness in the future will require new forms of resilience. As virtual reality, artificial intelligence, and immersive platforms expand, we must ensure that our inner lives remain grounded. Digital soulcraft will demand practices that anchor us in presence, preventing disorientation.

Creativity will flourish in new mediums. The future may bring tools we cannot yet imagine, but the essence of creativity will remain: the courage to express authentically. Digital soulcraft will invite us to use these tools not for spectacle but for meaning.

Connection will be the ultimate test. Will technology deepen our bonds or erode them? The answer depends on our choices. The future of digital soulcraft is a collective endeavor, a commitment to shaping technology in service of humanity.

16

Chapter 16: Crafting Community Online

Community is the soul's refuge, and in the digital age, it takes new forms. Online communities can be sources of support, creativity, and belonging, but they can also foster division. Digital soulcraft teaches us to craft communities with care.

Wellness within community requires safety. Spaces must be designed to protect against harm, to foster respect, and to nurture growth. When communities prioritize wellness, they become sanctuaries rather than battlegrounds.

Creativity thrives in community. Collaboration sparks innovation, and shared projects expand imagination. Digital communities can become workshops of the soul, places where individuals inspire one another to create boldly.

Connection is the essence of community. Beyond shared interests, true community offers solidarity, empathy, and mutual care. Digital soulcraft insists that communities are not merely networks but families of choice, woven together by intention.

17

Chapter 17: The Soul's Digital Legacy

Every click, every post, every creation contributes to a legacy. In the digital age, our souls leave traces that outlive us. Digital soulcraft asks: what kind of legacy do we wish to leave?

Wellness shapes legacy. A life lived with balance, with care for the inner world, leaves behind not only digital artifacts but also memories of presence. Wellness ensures that our legacy is not one of burnout but of vitality.

Creativity shapes legacy profoundly. The art we share, the stories we tell, the ideas we contribute — these become part of the collective archive. Creativity ensures that our legacy is not silence but song.

Connection completes legacy. The relationships we nurture, the kindness we extend, the communities we build — these are the soul's true inheritance. Digital soulcraft reminds us that legacy is not about permanence but about impact, about the ways our digital lives touch the lives of others.

www.ingramcontent.com/pod-product-compliance
Lightning Source LLC
Chambersburg PA
CBHW062309240926
51846CB00013B/934
9789788874928